AT THE WOODLINE

BOOKS BY PRESTON HORNBECK

State Lines

At the Woodline

AT THE WOODLINE

new poems

To Tommy,

You are a vital man.

Love you fiercly.

With Joy,

Prston

Gold & Light Publishing
Preston Hornbeck

This book is dedicated to
The Cageless Birds

He honors your colorless moments and celebrates
the turning from grayscale to living color.

— Melissa Helser

Contents

To Make a Heart a Home   *15*

Slowing Down   *17*

Wheat Fields   *19*

On the Nature of Daylight   *21*

Summer Walks   *23*

There, off the Trail   *25*

Pockets of Light   *27*

Where the Light Swells   *29*

All of the Bees   *31*

Those Gentle Steps   *33*

On the Winds of Morning   *35*

Ascension   *37*

Early   *39*

Wild Souls   *41*

Mourning Dove   *43*

Black Snake   *45*

Rhyme and Reason   *47*

Arrival   49

Never Stop Saying Goodbye   *51*

The Night I Scared the Fox   *53*

Blue Heron of the Night   *55*

The Night at the Bookstore in Greensboro   *57*

One Tiny Grasshopper   *59*

The Luna Moth   *61*

Remembering   *63*

The Day Will Be Well-Lit 65

Where Does the Soul Go? 67

If I Were to Look Into the Eyes of God 69

Red Cardinal *71*

Winter 1946 73

What Becomes of the Fireflies? *75*

After the Wave of Grief Has Passed 77

Songs of the Woods *79*

Here and There *80*

There and Here *81*

Unlikely Friendship 83

Dancing in the Field of the Soul *85*

As Easily as Flowers 87

Where We Rise and Fall 89

My Friend, Mary Oliver 91

Why I Write 93

White Owl 95

Black Bird *97*

Little Pearls *99*

Pines *101*

With the End of Autumn 103

Little Golden Birds 105

Under the Willow 107

Onwards Through Pale Mist 109

At the Woodline 111

Preface

Before these poems filled the pages of the book you now hold, they were found on slow walks down a gravel trail that traced a quiet pond in the woods of North Carolina. The lines were carefully scooped up one by one off the early morning dew and messily jotted in a journal. The poems came in like healing often does—slowly, over days, little by little—and ultimately became a collection that has forever marked me. And I am marked not only by the form the poems are in now, but by where they came from.

I believe we give value when we give our attention. As I made space for my heart to heal, I made a practice of keeping my eyes open to the beauty around me. Beauty, sadness, love, joy, grief—they can often all exist at once. The sun, the birds, a moment of missing a loved one, a steaming cup of coffee, the fog swirling above the water each morning, friendship, art, the basil plant in the garden. I paid attention to the things that sparked my curiosity, and I aimed to sit with those things in "long moments" to understand why they were affecting me; to give value.

Slowing down, being present, and allowing myself to be affected led to a heart full of gratitude and inspiration. As a result, writing poetry felt like a very natural response. And since the writing process was slow, the early versions of these poems felt more received than strived for. I am grateful for this. I understand that writing isn't always this way.

Of course, I am still only speaking of the first steps of the writing process. The state that is the initial idea, the spark of inspiration, the conception of each poem. While, for me, the first drafts of these poems each flowed out quite naturally, that sense of ease did not follow me into what came next—the laborious months of wrestling through the editing process. Yet, however difficult, the editing process gave the poems more depth. As far as I'm concerned, both the ease and the struggle are normal and usually necessary in creating anything beautiful or interesting.

The result of the inspired stillness and labor alike, I hope, is a collection of poems that provide little windows for you to look into and see the world around you differently.

Poetry is unlike any other form of art. There is no melody to carry the words or heard sound to determine the tone of voice. There is no visual art to lend a picture to see. Often, there is not even a clear storyline for a mind to follow. There are only the few words, carefully chosen, with so much weight placed upon them; so few words to carry the melody and tone, the imagery and story. And what a frighteningly wonderful challenge that is.

The goal is always to land in connection. This, I believe, is the reasons why poetry can be so powerful. Creative writing can be so much more than a form of self-expression. Self-expression alone is only the shallow shoreline of an ocean of reasons to write. There are much deeper places to go. And it is a sacred gift when the deep places in one's heart connect with the deep places in another. This is why we read. This is why we write.

So, wherever you find yourself today as you read these pages, I offer you my most sincere thanks for giving value to *At the Woodline*. Whether young or old, a new explorer of poetry or a well-versed voyager, my prayer is that the love and beauty I have experienced in my depths would be felt and shared by yours. That you would feel known. And that as you flip through, wade into, and linger in these pages, your heart would be reminded that it is worth beauty. So that you might feel more deeply connected to yourself, others, the world around you, and love. Because you're worth it.

— PH

To dive deeper into "At the Woodline", and discover more writing from Preston Hornbeck, scan the QR code above.

AT THE WOODLINE

To Make a Heart a Home

I walked in and
immediately noticed the light

dancing through the blinds,
casting shadow stairs,
climbing the wooden floor,
gold dust particles singing.

The room was waiting.
Like it was made for me. Waiting.
I leaned back in the wooden rocking chair,
closed my eyes, centered, and took a deep breath;

and there it was
everything I was
and everything I was becoming

waiting for me, unhurried.
In a house being made a home
I watched the light dance
and stayed.

Slowing Down

I left the hurry and took a walk.
And ambling down the gravel trail
was a yellow butterfly, turns out.

Mindless, yet perfectly thoughtful,
that gentle spirit.

His song drew me
and wooed me down to the swing where I sat,
where the water's reflection
then borrowed my attention.

He flew away, carrying his tune,
but I stayed, and my eyes drifted out
to the shadows,
those silhouettes draped by the swinging trees.

Those dark shapes climbed slowly up the dock.
And the day got hotter and hotter.
My eyes looked back down to the water,

down to that cool, deep soul at rest.
And as I stared, everything in the entire universe
began to make sense.

All of this happened on a whim,
in a long moment.

Wheat Fields

I am the little boy,
blonde hair hidden by the wheat stocks,
gently wrapped in the arms
of golden violin strings.

I am grown, running
through the shafts and into the light—struck
by wonder,
with brown hair blown back,
I feel

my face is soft again.
My gaze turns to the sky and the light swells.
Decades of life are connecting within.

I am staying.
The wind meets me
and we become reacquainted,
friends once more—

sharing tangible memories, laughing.
I am healing.

On the Nature of Daylight

The sun is waking up
to the fading songs of the birds
that called him forth
from his dark blue comforter

just beyond the long-fingered branches
to the east. Pouring through the trees,
a soft tapping at my window
inviting me to step outside. I respond,
lightly treading toward the light.

Then there is that beautiful feeling again—
the coolness of damp grass between my toes
and the warmth of light touching my face.

How happy I am to be alive for a sunrise.
This is a glory.

Summer Walks

Sometimes I walk through the dew
down to the water.
Other times, I walk the careful path.

Sometimes I bend down along the way,
and pluck a few basil leaves from the garden
to nibble on.
Other times, I simply pass.

I will say that usually, I do prefer
to feel the dew under my feet;
to take the trouble to reach for the leaves—

but there are many ways to conduct a prayer.

I just know that I want to walk hand-in-hand
with Delight forever.

Let's return to the Garden.

There, off the Trail

Near the walking trail,
I watched a squirrel frolic through the clover.
Upon hearing my footsteps moving in closer,
he hid behind a fence post.

We both waited patiently
for the other to move first—
what a silly squirrel, I thought!

All of him was hidden—all except that bushy tail.
Like a child that thinks you cannot see him
for the blanket over his head.

Weren't we all, at one time or another,
just like him? So afraid of the unknown—
so certain of hiding.

What has become of that child?
The one that frolicked and hid under blankets?

Don't say growing up has gotten the best of him.
I can still see him there, just behind the fence post.

Pockets of Light

It does not matter
how many leaves
dangle from
the countless trees—

inevitably,
I seem to find
the low-hanging light
peaking through the woodline

whenever I stop to notice it.
And there is always space to notice it.

Where the Light Swells

Over a black, silvery pond,
over waters still as ice—
The breath of God hovers.

It is the break of daylight,
where the light swells.

With warmth on my skin,
and the unchangeable hope of redemption
in my heart.
This is dawn.

With glorious earth
wrapped in golden morning
by sun and song.
This is dawn.

The silent messenger to the earth,
saying that everything matters.
This is dawn.

Beholding us, as we begin to see clearly—
beholding us, we begin to see—

And this is the start of the song
that all of creation
has long awaited.

All of the Bees

You beautiful bees—
when did I become so afraid of you?
I cannot know you if I cannot sit with you.

For so long I have run.
Flight
at the sound of a buzz
was a learned tendency.
Surely you understand?

Childlike curiosity once carried me—

perhaps I learned fear
at eight years old
when I was stung.

Today, in a little effort
to restore my gentle soul,
I will not run.

I will be
in the garden
sitting with you again.
Until the fear of the sting
has faded, and faded,
and faded.
And I become still like the flowers
you call your friends.

Maybe I too will bloom
because of my choice to stay.

Sweet nectar of unusual sorts.

Those Gentle Steps

At sunrise I walked through the dew
down to the garden beds
to find the bluebirds, already singing
and making nests.

Then I heard a rustle from the blueberry bushes.
I slowly approached.

A bluebird eating blueberries—what a funny thought,
I thought to myself.
The bluebird did not think so.
She flew away

and her friends all stopped singing.
Then, I was alone in the garden
with no song to hear.

Sometimes fear drives us away, too.
None of us wants to lose to fear.
Though, sometimes we do.

But oh, how glorious it is
when we hear those gentle steps
approaching us in the Garden;

when we are tempted to run
and choose to stay.

On the Winds of Morning

Just this morning
I heard the wind calling me again.

Come, follow me! said it.

And, curious bird I've become,
I went.

I went and I flew!
Like I've done a hundred times over now—
with all of their eyes still watching.

Was I to stay where I was comfortably dying?
Heaven forbid they say I slipped from the faith.
As if they could judge the heart of man.
As if they should.

No, soaring only seems bewildering
through the lens of bitterness.

As for me and my house,
we will befriend the wind,
learn her lovely secrets,
give in.

Ascension

There is a silvery fog swirling
upon the water, poised and sweet.
Spinning like a ballet dancer,
making little ripples
with each step.

The spotlight sun is rising behind her.
And my heart is leaping with joy,
over and over again.

And the orange fire of a new horizon
goes on
ripping apart the seams of earth and sky.
Bringing with it every waking beautiful thing.

Oh, to be under a new morning's sun—
where everything is lifted,
and settles in a warm glow.

To sit and watch with fire in my eyes—
within the array of light, of dancing—

it is almost heavenly, this place
where nature delights in sharing secrets.

Early

Beneath the weeping willow
the burning red rose early—
uncharacteristically so,
before the birds started singing.

A new sun stared at me—
as did its reflection
upon the water's surface.

It was as if the heavens had fixed
their two bright eyes
upon mine.

And the birds were not yet singing
but I was.

Wild Souls

We are the wild souls
who hide our hearts in plain sight.
Drawn to the beauty in nature,
wrapped warmly
in her delight.

We are the wild souls—
the feet that tread gently, seemingly without cause.
It is not so.
That gentle tread has taken practice—
it takes time to unlearn the weighty *shoulds*.

But we are the wild souls—
every step, eternally keeping pace with wonder—
forfeiting our fears in a graceful exchange;

the souls for which home abounds
and lost is lost.

Mourning Dove

Down past the blackberry bushes
is where we've found our path,
just off the gravel road
through the fine droplet-dripped grass.

Where sunlight only dreams
of what it'll soon become.
Where pines and rose petals meet
at the waterfront.

How long can sunrise last here—with the one I love?
Forever, I suppose. Alas,
comes the call of the mourning dove:
It is time to fly. Won't you be joining me?

I am! I am!

Black Snake

I'll tell you a true story
of when, down by the garden shed,
came the rats and rabbits
eating all the carrots and cabbage.

The men and women
sought to handle the matter
with poison, seals, and traps.

Little good did they do—the rodents did not
bite the bait.
Nature solemnly shook her head,

my dear, uncomfortable humans, wait.

Then came the black snake,
neither poisonous nor revered,
and soon,
all of the little thieves of the garden were cleared.

What do you make of this?

The black snake now has a new home
within and about the garden shed.
And the humans have learned reverence.

Both are being fed.

Rhyme and Reason

I believe, like each of us,
I too was made for something great.

At this point, what greatness this is,
I do not know.

But when I consider the sunrise before me,
the steaming cup of coffee in my hand,
the not so small joy of writing with my favorite pen;

When I see the children,
laughing and running through the garden;
When I sense the delight and the smile of God—

then I wonder,
has it always been as simple as this?

Arrival

I love the sound your feet make
when they slightly scoot across the tops
of the gravel rocks

as you follow the guideposts
down to the water;
to the place
where we meet so often.

Yes, the sound
of your feet coming—
the sound of your arrival
is my favorite
poetry.

Never Stop Saying Goodbye

The sudden weight of reality
hit me. Dripping, dropping,
each word fell heavy
on my heart—

You'll never stop saying goodbye.
Teardrops filling his eyes,
to match my own
slowly
swelling
rise.

Until the waters within me
began to crack
the damned blockade I'd built
to keep me safe and presentable.

His white beard and wrinkled skin
were well acquainted with these waters.
He rested his hand upon my shoulder.

You'll always miss him.
You'll always be letting go.
There's no easy way through it—you'll always be
saying goodbye.
And it's one of the hardest things on earth.

A rip of life, tears burst forth,
through my denying soul.
Restoring my humanity, reminding me
of our frailty.
Something beyond words at work,
making me whole.

And we became cold rivers—
overflowing the banks of sorrow,
grief washing our eyes clearer and clearer.

Bluer from the water
than I've ever been before
at the place where pain and loss
coincide with affection and admiration.

Pouring, rushing,
as an hour passed
on the shores
of love and longing.

The Night I Scared the Fox

On the road
beaming lights show
a burnt orange tail
swiftly darting home.
I have scared the fox straight into the bushes.

He will get over this fear.
We both will.

I drive home. Then,
parked under speckled stars
spark the lightning bugs—all across the farm.
From the open field to the tree line,
down the hill, and over the pond—
like little flashes of hope
until we reach dawn.

And we will reach dawn.

For now, I am the sojourner of the night
following every sacred light,
chasing every scared fox back home,

where the night sky
lies down quietly
between the pine tops and powerlines,
and rests her head,
where the racing energy stops.

Blue Heron of the Night

Under a blanket of stars
the Blue Heron covered
lies awake.

Tucked into the branches of his tree for the night,
looking down into the reflecting silver specks,
unable to sleep.

Do we all feel the same things?
Do we all long for love?

Maybe the Heron is awake
only to soak in the silence
found between dusk and dawn.

It must be exhausting—
to feel like the only one of your kind—
surrounded by beautiful songs
from dozens of other birds.

And the Blue Heron is not like the sparrows,
robins, or the finches—he is only one.
He is just the Heron.
Oh, Blue Heron of the night,
how did you get here,
sleeping alone, so high up in that tree?

Regardless of how, he is there.
Unknowingly, beautiful as ever.
Maybe tomorrow he will feel better.

For now, he will lie awake, wide awake.
Perfectly still, with his restless heart inside him.

The Night at the Bookstore in Greensboro

At this point, there are times
when I think to myself in sheer
verse and rhyme.

And I must stop myself
and ask myself,
"Is this *me* thinking?
Or, is there something to be said?"
I almost never know in the moment.

I was thinking in verse, when,
at the bookstore in Greensboro,
I exchanged my company of friends for poems.
It was Mary Oliver, Robert Frost, others that
stole me away.
And I fell into the pages, utterly captivated.

Then, to my surprise,
ten minutes, or thirty, or an hour later,
when I looked back up
I found that my other friends were lost.
Or it was I, the one who stayed too long—

so it was I.
And I tried to act like I was content as I smiled
politely at the clerk.
I heard the bell ring as I walked out the door, alone.

On an evening stroll in the city,
with new books of poetry in my bag—
joy in one hand,
then, there was the other.

One Tiny Grasshopper

I remembered to close the door behind me
as I walked inside.

Still, a breeze of summer night
remembered before me,
and rushed in quickly
to close the door before I could,
but not before
one tiny grasshopper could jump in safely.

It all happened so quickly.
Then, in the entry, there sat this grasshopper.
Beady-eyed, arched legs on my bookshelf,
perfectly at rest, settled, at home.

This was not a gentle, poetic moment.
I was not amused.
So I grabbed a book—
but I could not bring myself
to fault his innocence.

So I took my book, along with my
burnt-orange book bag,
and stole out the door unnoticed.
What became of the grasshopper I cannot say.

I left him to skim the other books as he pleased,
while I ran away—far away from him,
and kept running.

The Luna Moth

There she lay beneath the hardwood trees,
with skin thinner than birch leaves,
with wings of mint green,
her little sails at rest in the brown dirt.

I picked her up, admiring
her wings' curves and their little eyes.
But with her in hand I mostly felt
the sad absence of life.

Eleven months she waited
for ten days to live.
And now she seemed so perfect,
yet lay limp, motionless.

I wonder if at the end she was content.

But what more could she have wanted?
She had cocooned and survived,
sailed the wind of a few summer nights—
the slowest, most splendid streak across the navy
you'd ever seen—
and then she set her little self down softly.

Was death sad for her?
It is to me.
I wanted more. Time is all too brief.

I hope
the last week of August
was everything she'd dreamt it'd be.

Remembering

You would not believe
what I saw the other day.
Then again, hopefully, you might—

but I noticed that outside, there was a glowing
coming from the field.

And through the trees I could see
that the field, at least in part,
was consumed!

Heavenly fire!—
angels!—or glory!—

what it was I cannot say.
But I prayed an old prayer—

oh, how I long
to unforget
what I seem to have forgotten
so very long ago.

To go back to the abundance,
to the first field of light.

The Day Will Be Well-Lit

He's at it again,
with his bright red chest pressed out
and notes flying
before the sun has begun to climb the sky.

Robins give little mind to your sleep patterns—
they were born to sing.
And you—

sometimes you must wake up earlier
than you wished—
and sometimes you must walk farther
than you hoped
to find what it is you were born for.

But can we figure out, in a few short decades,
the purpose of our lives?
Certainly that is an awful lot of pressure.

Maybe it happens upon us.
Maybe it is a long-sought treasure.
Or, maybe, sure as the sun,
it has been there all along,
too wide and generous and forgiving
for us to recognize.

Don't believe the illusion
that you could have done better
or lessened your troubles
with a more suitable route—as if your past
could be changed.

Let the night be the night.
But the day—the day will be well-lit.
And I've never seen a delay in daylight
keep a robin from singing.

Where Does the Soul Go?

At the end of the road,
when the pale light has swollen and shut—

when the body has laid down for its last lie,
to sleep in the dark ground,
touching the cold sleep of death—

the spirit still soars.

Up into the sky—crying,
Finally! Show me glory!
How happy is he!

And the body toils no longer. This is his long rest.

But what becomes of the soul?
The mind, the will, the emotions—
the meeting place of body and spirit,
could anyone know where he is to go?

And what of his unanswered questions?
The doubts, the fears, the lack—these must die
when we pass.

But is the soul not more alive than the body itself?
Or, are we not to think, will, or feel any longer?
How tragic!
Something more does come—

Still, how could we know?
We cannot.

Souls are not the talk of certainty—
but, isn't this important?
Isn't this nearly everything?

So where does the soul go
when he is no longer within body, within spirit?

If I Were to Look Into the Eyes of God

If I were to look into the eyes of God
I suppose I would no longer need to search.
There would be no need to seek beauty
in the ocean, poetry, places—

for now, I only see specks lit,
incomparably small glimmers
of what is contained within
those twin galaxies.
Still, remarkable specks of those twin galaxies.

But there is a difference between seeing
and beholding. Shooting stars and permanent light.

Yes, if I were to look into the eyes of God,
and see those steady flames burning bright,
consuming every desire,
where all that is left is worship,

I believe I'd find every ocean, poem, place—
everything I was made for and more—
all contained within those two eyes,
wild as water, beautiful as a flame—those glimmers
fixed on me.

Oh, ephemeral beauty. It has this way
of satisfying the deepest longing of my heart,
and yet, still managing to leave it utterly a mess,
longing for more.

A kind of kindly taunt that forever says,
I think you're the loveliest thing alive.
Won't you come see me again?

Red Cardinal

Red Cardinal of the pines,
like hope dressed in a little red coat
sitting still before me—unable to hide
within the mess of needles and cones.

You are teaching me.
In stillness, I'm listening.
In stillness, I'm finding you.

No, you will not sing *for* me.
But still, I am listening.
And though I cannot yet hear a song,
I can see you there.

In the woods, waiting,
watching from within the shadows.
Not singing a piercing song,
but always there,
breathing.

Breathing inside that coat of fire.
That red flame seen through the thickest trees—

sitting, gleaming.
Staring back at me,
unafraid of the dark.

Winter 1946
In response to the painting by Andrew Wyeth

The hill is breathing.
It is not fast or slow;
It is breath.

The wind is ceasing.
It does not come or go,
it is dead.

And the beating heart thuds like it is the only noise
left on earth.
Of course, it is not—
mine beats too—
How utterly devastating
and world-shattering it is then,
when the breathing hill
stops.

Where has that playful drum gone? Beating
with all its might—
the only thuds left
are my muddy boots,
as I pant and rage
down the hill—
a painful, painful sight.

What Becomes of the Fireflies?

Fragile fireflies, angels of the night,
dwindling lights signifying summer's end—
hundreds of deft flickers of fire,
quietly disappearing with the light of dusk.

Sometimes *goodbye* doesn't feel like enough.

This is sadness,
the waning cluster told me.
But reminiscing reminds us we've held the beautiful.

Can we see the majesty in a flash?
Can we make a moment last forever?
This whole world is in a flutter.

It must be a noble thing
to sit and behold
flashes of light in the dark
when all along we know the light won't last.

After the Wave of Grief Has Passed

The grey silk sheets above the earth
have been rolled back,
and behind the elms, the oaks,
and the soft maples,

shaken, but still standing, we are
found fixed as stones in the dirt, and still gazing
upwards, through newly spotted, floodlit, pink
cotton tuft appearing.

Fly, fly, fly, away—beastly, puffy cheeks of sky.
There can be no more rain today.
It has had its time.

Now is the move from groaning to gloaming.
They can exist within a moment together—
can't you feel the cool wind blowing?
Wrapping its kind arms around my body.

And now I can lift my heavy head again—
something has been lifted from me—
and there is that orange ball of fire
falling in the distance.

Songs of the Woods

When it comes to glory,
beyond the woodline,
there seems to be no end.

The woods live their whole life a home,
with treetops spiraling upwards,
creating shelters, providing safe spaces to grow.

Where, perched in their pews,
the birds sing a bright chorus.
So happy—the peculiar saints of the forest.
Just this morning, I witnessed two of them
dancing on a branch.

There are angels, too, singing
sunbeams of light fluttering through
the tall, tall, green-leafed canopy above.

There are new songs being sung here every morning.
The woods are always singing,
inviting us to listen, to join in,
to take our place.

Here and There

You can often find me running off
through the woodline
and sitting down by the pond.

Not to hide;
rather, to return.

My friends live here—
as well as there.

Though I must admit I quite prefer
grassy moss to cold tiles beneath toes;
an intimate breeze over air conditioning;
and a reflection that ripples and waves in
the water, opposed to the prosaic stare
of a mirror.

And if it were not for the pesky sweat bees,
I'd never leave.

There and Here

Nearly 20 minutes ago I wrote a poem
down by the pond.

Then the sweat bees came around,
drawn to my salt,
and they were too much for me to take.

So I ran through the woodline,
up the hill and over the roots,
back to the quiet cabin.

I walked in,
luxuriated in the fuzz of a Moroccan rug
beneath my toes,
opened the windows,
caught myself smiling as I passed by the mirror,
and reclined on the couch. But then

I began daydreaming again
about those silly little metallic kings and queens,
yellow stripes crowded together, flocking to life.

An Unlikely Friendship

The clock's hands have stopped.

My hands have stopped, too.

Aren't we becoming good friends,

time and I?

Dancing in the Field of the Soul

There is a field that only bare feet can know.
It is a place the spirit loves to go.

To get there, you must go out
from beyond the hardwood maple and soft carpet
floors. And out beyond the doors that hide them.

You must glide over
all the small sharp gravel rocks,
and every prickly wood chip
that makes you want to stop.

You must twirl out over the lush green giant,
the mighty hill—up until finally,
just past the spot the tomatoes,
blueberries, and wildflowers grow,
you reach the sacred, wild field of the soul;

the soft meadow of the night
in secret soliloquies dressed;
the place where tired hearts
and sore feet can rest.

And if you find this field,
then you know you have what it takes—
you are one of those brave enough
to run, to dance, to feel the ache.

Is it the heart or the toes that first learn to leap?
And which of the two has the audacious courage
to follow?

Maybe the body and the spirit
were made to dance together
in the wild field of the soul.

As Easily as Flowers

The green towers are dancing again,
leanly swaying back and forth
as easily as flowers.

And without a sound,
their tiny lifeboats
descend down, and slowly lower to the ground.

Falling for moments, and twirling in tiny tornados,
one by one they slip away
from everything they've known.

What courage.

Where We Rise and Fall

On this perfectly overcast autumn day,
with clouds, tall golden grass, and many other
living things existing,
rising and falling,

the bees put their noses to the huckleberries,
the squirrels leap through the trees,
and we spread out a blanket to sit and read
in the hidden field.

It took us a long time to get here.

Lucas says the grass is taller than usual.
Ben says he doesn't much mind.
It is fall now, after all, and it'll all soon die.

But we are here now.
Not yet gone—we are here.

We read our books, sitting together in silence.

My heart beats slowly,
my chest rising and falling.

My Friend, Mary Oliver

My friend, Mary Oliver, died in January.

It deeply pains me that we did not meet
until afterward, in May.

But I read her pages all summer, all fall.

And while we have not known each other long—
true—still, that crazy old woman has become one
of my dearest companions.

So dear, that I pray for others
to feel the same belonging in my words
that I have found in hers.

If you are one who can
I hope you do.

We're not far-fetched or far off.
Only a wander through the woodline away,
where the light is always more ambitious to find us
than we are it.

I hope you'll join us.

Why I Write

My writing
has become truer to who
I am
with time, with practice.

And I suppose
this will always be
true—as long as I continue
to lean into
honesty, vulnerability, curiosity.

Those are the golden keys
that swing wide the red doors of the heart,
that allow access to words that matter,
to poetry.

And I am learning to write as my heart beats—
for nearness—

so I will give my best words for her.
Pumping honest blood—
she can have my aching lines
and my best moments.

But all they could ever mean is this:
there was something significant, and I felt it.

And I long for wholehearted emotions,
for conviction, for delight.
And I long to feel purpose and meaning,
for connection and healing.

And, don't we all?
Don't we all, most of all, want love?

To live inside the house of love,
to live inside, and live inside.

And in all the uproars—
something significant, and we felt it.

White Owl

I.

I will watch carefully
for the White Owl,
on the trails where moonbeams peer through trees.

Though under this summer's crescent she soars unseen,
I will continue to wait patiently.

Dare I say, I do believe, my eyes will behold her
and her noble shadow streaking through the interstices
before this fall.

She isn't far from me.

II.

The summer passed, and then the fall.
I moved away and I never saw the White Owl.

It hurts my heart to know
such beauty could exist, but be missed.

Should I have looked more?
I was so determined to see that stunning bird.

Perhaps even our resoluteness does not make us God.
Maybe it is best I missed her.

Maybe I'll see her yet.

Black Bird

Oddly, there is a crow walking.
Slow-moving, seemingly unaware. I know,
her feet were made for more than gravel.

Yet, here she is,
meandering the little grey rocks.
I know it's rude
but I can't help but stare
at her little wirey legs; her searching eyes,
curious, beady and intellegent.

And how gorgeous is that black beak,
so precisely shaped, now scouring over
yesterday's busted black trash bags,
settling for leftovers.

This is injustice.
She was gifted to make brilliant cursive strokes
upon the blank blue pages above.
How can I help her
lift her ink-wings to the sky once more?

The world needs more of her tales of wisdom.
Oh, misinterpreted mystery of magnificence.

You are the precious one with the depths of the
starry night in each feather. And what has cast
you down cannot hold you back forever.

There is no other
that has what you have to offer.

The world is aching to see you fly.

Little Pearls

Little pearls
from the ocean floor of heaven

drip down through the clouds
and rip through the trees.

The branches catch most of the droplets,
but the naughty ones catch Blake's feet.

Let the rain fall, if it must.
The poets will still speak.

Pines

The fog rolled in between the pines.
Unplanned, floating in
over the early morning field.

A friend said he was frustrated
because we were behind.

I expressed that I was awfully sorry about that,
and I thought that perhaps
I might be irritated too.

But then I looked out the car window
and saw the trees standing there,
letting the fog pass through them;
telling me otherwise.

With the End of Autumn

Many moons had come and gone,
and it had been a while since I'd embarked
into the fields of poetry.
And I was frustrated with myself
because writers are to write,
are they not?

Then came the bumble bee,
crawling slowly
as she whispered to me
that it was time for her long sleep,
as happens.

She quietly urged me to join her.
She closed her eyes and took one deep breath,
let out a small sigh, and slipped off—
like the flowers had also done.

And still, I did not want to let go
of my expectations—the dreadful weight
of producing, to be a constant.

But the bees and flowers
will all return.
The world will be
a wonder once more.
And I suppose that tiny deaths are necessary
for revival in spring.

Yes, there are seasons for poetry, as there are
for any other thing.

Little Golden Birds

All of our little golden birds
have flown from our branches
to join their brothers and sisters
waiting, at rest on the sleepy ground.

The cold has pushed them into transition.
And courageously they've gone—while,
simultaneously, our roots have gone on, too,
descending down.

And we all will fall.
Like leaves from splendor,
or roots to strength.

Our beds are made in the times of transition,
and we lie on the beds we make.

So let us reach our arms to the heavens
even—no, especially—when we have
no gold to show.
And let our roots ever expand in winter.

There is purpose in every breath
of our wind-swept bodies.

Under the Willow

This land holds so many memories.

On the square dock,
a cherished few are resting—and
under the dead willow tree, a handful of others.
Upon the bridge there live two more memories.
And then there, down at our favorite spot,
there reside too many to recall.

Forget about me trying to mention
all of the others that could be found
on a stroll down the gravel trail,
or in a pass through the field that connects it all.

Right now, I am remembering.
But this land always remembers.
She has become my friend.

And I will go on to another life,
one day die. And still,
she will be here, tending to the souls
busy blazing their trails.

Yes, long after I'm gone,
maybe even then
we'll still be old friends—
swinging back and forth
in the dance of remembering

like we used to, under the willow,
before she too
lived forever.

Onwards Through Pale Mist

There could be war paint on his cheeks.
It might as well be blood that stains his skin.
As he walks past the familiar waters a final time—
not to return here again.

His hair, now long and slicked back.
His beard now runs past his chin.
These lands that have watched
his continual growings
will no longer witness them.

And the crane has yet to fly away
from her beloved silver pond;
she has yet to venture through the valley
carrying the living colors of fall.

But the singing birds will all fly away.
And the crane will soar.

With rolling tears he ties
his boot laces here a final time.
And with a full heart he whispers farewell.

Accepting this departure,
moving onwards through the pale mist
like the red cardinal through the white clouds—
on the wings of morning with woodland scent.

At the Woodline

When the night goes out
and there comes again that not-subtle flame
over the horizon—
inching its way forward,
torching the forest with light,
making the cold woods warm again.

And the earth becomes something else
under the luminescence of that unbridled glow.

When here am I in the middle of it.
With sun lines being drawn around me,
with the darkest places being etched away
by the kindest scratches of light,
with grayscale transformed to living color.

And I run wildly through the woods,
touched by light, filled by its brilliant brightness.

Acknowledgments

I would like to thank Jonathan and Melissa Helser, The Cageless Birds, and my fellow 18 Inch Journey alumni. Thank you for being with me in joy and sorrow; celebration and stillness; messes and moments of beauty alike. Thank you for sharing your heart with me and for valuing mine. You've taught me so much about love.

Thank you, Jake Stevens. My eyes swell with tears of gratitude as I stop to remember how you've walked with me. Thank you, Justina Stevens, Chris Miller, Jessie Miller, Phyllis Unkefer, Allie Sampson, JD Gravitt, Martha McRae, Molly Skaggs, Joel Case, Emily Pell, and Erica Allen for teaching me how to fight for my heart and voice. Thank you, Papa Ken, Cade Garlock, Nic Farley, Gabriel Ramerez, Chanelle Hall, and the rest of the Cageless Birds for loving me deeply. Each of you has impacted my life significantly.

Thank you, Blake Steen, for giving this collection of poems your full heart. You are a faithful and steadfast editor. Thank you for standing at my side and guarding my flank. The world is brighter because of the light of your life and I am proud to call you friend. Thank you, Rachel Yumi Chung and Valina Yen, for your dedication to crafting a beautiful and meaningful book cover. Your impact on this collection is substantial.

Thank you, Gold & Light, Carmen Miller, Abigail Taylor, Dolores James, Josiah Armstrong, and friends who have helped to make publishing a reality. And to my mom, sisters, family, friends, leaders, and community that walk with me day in and day out—who love me as I am and believe in who I am becoming—thank you, thank you, thank you. I am grateful.

— PH